GW00492558

TO

ASHLEY,

FROM

Heather Stewart

DATE

June 2000.

SUCCESS

SUCCESS

THE SOURCE
OF SUCCESS

For who is God besides the Lord? And who is the Rock except our God? It is God who arms me with strength and makes my way perfect. He makes my feet like the feet of a deer; he enables me to stand on the heights.

2 SAMUEL 22:32-34

May our lives be
illumined
by the steady radiance
renewed daily,
of a wonder,
the Source of which
is beyond reason.

DAG HAMMERSKJÖLD

There are two lives we live,
one before God alone, and
one before others. As we draw
our strength from God we are
enabled to live successfully
before others.

ROY LESSIN

We discover the most
satisfying success when
we remember that the value
of working hard and doing
good things is not based on
their numbers and excellence,
but comes from the love of
God which prompts us
to do these things.

Commit to the Lord whatever you do, and your plans will succeed.

PROVERBS 16:3

The secret of success is constancy of purpose.

BENJAMIN DISRAELI

*A*ligning our life with God's purpose
for us gives a sense of destiny.... It gives
form and direction to our life.

JEAN FLEMING

Our purpose here
is to glorify God.
It is in our daily
relationship with
Him that we find
ultimate success,
for this has
eternity in it.

It's not possible for a person to succeed— I'm talking about eternal success— without heaven's help.

JOHN 3:27 MSG

If I'm not free to fail, I'm not free to take risks, and everything in life that's worth doing involves a willingness to take a risk. If true success is found in my willingness to take risks, then I know God offers an abundant supply of all I need. I do not have to "succeed," only dare to try. Ultimate success comes from following God and has nothing to do with success as the world sees success.

Man is the greatest marvel
in the universe. Not because
his heart beats forty million
times a year, driving the
bloodstream a distance of
over sixty thousand miles in
that time; not because of his
successes, his cleverness,
or his personality; but
because he may walk
and talk with God.

ROY LESSIN

Be still, and know
that I am God.

PSALM 46:10

And the Lord God formed
man of the dust of the ground,
and breathed into his nostrils
the breath of life; and man
became a living soul.

GENESIS 2:7

Get the pattern of your life
from God, then go about your
work and be yourself.

PHILLIPS BROOKS

$\mathbb{T}$*he resource from which God gives
is boundless, measureless, unlimited,
unending, abundant, and eternal.*

JACK HAYFORD

The kind of success
that counts comes
from living by inner
purpose, rather than
by outer pressures.

The secrets of success unfold, one by one, to the person who walks near enough to God to hear the secrets He has to impart.

THE
FOUNDATION
FOR SUCCESS

The answer for satisfying living...lies not in organizing, managing, or controlling life, but in focusing life.... Life is simplified when there is one center, one reason, one motivation, one direction and purpose.

JEAN FLEMING

Delight yourself in the Lord
and he will give you the
desires of your heart.

PSALM 37:4

A man's dreams are an
index to his greatness.

ZABOK RABINOWITZ

When a man feels throbbing within him the power to do what he undertakes as well as it can possibly be done, this is happiness, this is success.

ORISON SWETT MARDEN

We grow great by dreams. All big men are dreamers.

WOODROW WILSON

God has not called me to be successful;
He has called me to be faithful.

MOTHER TERESA

To have faith is to have wings.

JAMES M. BARRIE

$\mathbb{F}$aith risks everything...it's a radical willingness to believe that with God all things are possible. As you begin trying to do what once seemed so impossible, the light of success will dawn upon you, shining brightly with rewards you never could've imagined.

Splendid things have been achieved by those who dared to accept God's gift of grace, believing that His living inside of them was superior to any circumstance.

Ambition is that grit in the soul which creates disenchantment with the ordinary and puts the dare into dreams.

MAX LUCADO

THE
EXPRESSION
OF SUCCESS

The really great
man is the man who
makes everyone
feel great.

G. K. CHESTERTON

He has achieved success who has lived well; laughed often and loved much; who has gained the respect of intelligent men and the love of little children; who has filled his niche and accomplished his task; who has left the world better than he found it, whether by an improved poppy, a perfect poem or a rescued soul; who has never lacked appreciation of earth's beauty, or failed to express it; who has always looked for the best in others and given the best he had; whose life was an inspiration; whose memory a benediction.

BESSIE ANDERSON STANLEY

Remember you will not always win. Some day, the most resourceful individual will taste defeat. But there is, in this case, always tomorrow—after you have done your best to achieve success today.

MAXWELL MALTZ

It is better to deserve honors
and not have them than
to have them and not
deserve them.

MARK TWAIN

A great secret of success is to
go through life as a man who
never gets used up.

ALBERT SCHWEITZER

The price of success is hard work, dedication to the job at hand, and the determination that whether we win or lose, we have applied the best of ourselves to the task at hand.

VINCE LOMBARDI

We can be so sure that every detail in our lives of love for God is worked into something good. God knew what he was doing from the very beginning. He decided from the outset to shape the lives of those who love him.

ROMANS 8:28-29 MSG

Take time to impress love upon
people's hearts and you will leave
behind a legacy of what a truly
successful life means.

Only the life lived for others
is a life worthwhile.

ALBERT EINSTEIN

The quality of a man's life
is in direct proportion to his
commitment to excellence,
regardless of his chosen
field of endeavor.

VINCE LOMBARDI

Excellence is to do a
common thing in an
uncommon way.

BOOKER T. WASHINGTON

I *do not think there is any*
other quality so essential to
success of any kind as the
quality of perseverance.
It overcomes almost
everything, even nature.

JOHN D. ROCKEFELLER, JR.

The reward of a thing well done is to have done it.

RALPH WALDO EMERSON

When we have done our best, we should wait the result in peace.

J. LUBBOCK

Success is fulfilling the purpose for which something was made. A plane would be a failure if it couldn't fly; a boat would be a failure if it didn't float. Our highest purpose is to know God and be reflections of Him to others. When our feet are walking this path, we are on the high road to success.

ROY LESSIN

BEHIND THE SCENE

"I paint because I feel that's what God wants me to do with the talent He's given me. It's not only a pleasure, but also an act of reverence to paint what I see around me," says Scott Kennedy. A Colorado native and well-known wilderness artist, Kennedy sets the scene for the painting used on this product.

"On the Heights"

This painting, more than any other, shows how the work of Maxfield Parrish has influenced my own work. It is what I term a surreal or dream-like landscape. It may remind you of a place you know, or more accurately, evoke a feeling through your memories of that certain place.

The idea for it came from the Bible. A verse in Psalm 18 says, "He makes my feet like the feet of a deer and enables me to stand on the heights."

In the painting, there are many layers of glazed color that push the limits of reality in nature. The overall lighting moves from darker tones in the foreground to lighter tones in the distant background, hopefully creating a broad sense of depth.